On the First Day of School

A Sing-Along Story

Sing to the tune of "The Twelve Days of Christmas."

A Publication of the World Language Division

Story written by: Elly Schottman

Director of Product Development: Judith M. Bittinger

Executive Editor: Elinor Chamas

Editorial Development: Judith M Bittinger, Susan Hooper, Kathleen M. Smith

Production/Manufacturing: James W. Gibbons

Cover and Text Design/Art Direction: Taurins Design Associates, New York

Illustrator: Yvonne Cathcart

ISBN 0-201-85331-0

1 2 3 4 5 6 7 8 9 10-WR-99 98 97 96 95

Addison-Wesley Publishing Company

3

On the first day of school,
I brought along with me
a monkey named Mr. Wiggly.

5

On the second day of school,
I brought along with me
2 talking toucans and
a monkey named Mr. Wiggly.

Today is Wednesday. How many Wednesdays are there in September?

September
S M T W Th F
            1 2 3 4
5
6 7 8 9 10 11 12
13 14 15 16 17 18 19
20 21 22 23 24 25 26
27 28 29 30

On the third day of school,
I brought along with me
    3 hopping hippos,
    2 talking toucans and
    a monkey named Mr. Wiggly.

How many
times can you
hop in ten
seconds?

| Henry Hippo | Paola |

9

On the fourth day of school,
I brought along with me
    4 leaping llamas,
    3 hopping hippos,
    2 talking toucans and
    a monkey named Mr. Wiggly.

Today is
Thursday.
Come to the
book fair
in the
cafeteria

11

On the fifth day of school,
I brought along with me
5 singing seals,
4 leaping llamas,

3 hopping hippos,
2 talking toucans and
a monkey named Mr. Wiggly.